Good Success

God's Blueprint for Successful Living

DeAndre M. Riley

Good Success: God's Blueprint for Successful Living

Copyright © 2016 Deandre M. Riley

Published by Deandre M. Riley

All rights reserved.

ISBN: 0692727582 | ISBN-13: 9780692727584

All scripture quotations are taken from the King James Version of the Bible, unless otherwise noted. Copyright © 1977, 1984, 2991 by Thomas Nelson, Inc. and from The Message. Copyright © 1993, 1994, 1995, 1996, 2000, 2001, 2002. Used by permission of NavPress Publishing Group

Cover Design: Mann Made Productions, LLC

Interior Design: Sow Graphics & Publications, LLC

Edited by Tenita C. Johnson of So It Is Written LLC.

Printed in the United States of America

ALL RIGHTS RESERVED

No part of this book may be reproduced in any form or by any electronic or mechanical means, including information storage and retrieval systems, without written permission from the publisher or author, except in the case of a reviewer, who may quote brief passages embodied in critical articles or in a review.

DEDICATION

I dedicate this book to DeAndre, Jr., Darren Marvin and Serenity Michelle. My prayer is for you to find good success in your lives.

CONTENTS

Dedication

Acknowledgements

Introduction To Good Success i

The Blueprint 1

The First "S" – Strength 13

"U" – Unity 25

The First "C" – Courage 33

The Second "C" - Contentment 47

"E" – Education (Knowledge) 57

The Second "S" – Selective (Be Selective) 73

The Third "S" – Salvation 87

Living The Good Success Life 101

Share The Wealth 111

About The Author 116

ACKNOWLEDGEMENTS

I still pinch myself sometimes when I think about being an author. I have to remind myself that I am not dreaming. It's a true joy to impact the lives of many through words. Therefore, I have made the commitment to continue to write as long as God gives me something to say.

First and foremost, I thank God for the ability to compile my thoughts and ideas into a book. Secondly, I thank you for supporting my work. Without your support, my message will never be heard. I am only as great as the people who support me.

I understand that I can only do so much by myself. In order to accomplish this type of undertaking, I need the assistance of many others. Thank you to the editorial guru who helps bring my writing to life, Tenita "Bestseller Johnson. Thank you for allowing me to ask you a hundred questions as it relates to the editing and book writing process.

To my family, friends and church family, your love, encouragement and continued support means everything to me. Thank you to my grandmother and grandfather who continue to exhibit strength, commitment and love. Thank you to my pastor, Daniel Grandberry, for your wisdom and support. Words fail me when I attempt to explain the impact you have had on my life. To the family that I have been fortunate to marry into, the Darby Family, my life is committed to making sure I do everything I can to show you that I appreciate your love and support to me and Porsha. To my children, Serenity Michelle and DeAndre, Jr., being a parent is one of the toughest, yet fulfilling responsibilities in the world. I count it a blessing to be your dad, and I will continue to do everything in my power to give you the best life.

Lastly, to my wife, my rib, my biggest cheerleader, I am a living witness of Proverbs 18:22 (ESV): *He who finds a wife a good thing and obtains favor from the Lord.* Thank you for your love along with your undying commitment to what we have built and are yet working to build. I love you always and forever. I'm blessed to live the *good success* life with you!

"This Book of the Law shall not depart from your mouth, but you shall meditate on it day and night, so that you may be careful to do according to all that is written in it. For then you will make your way prosperous, and then you will have good success.

(Joshua 1:8 ESV)

INTRODUCTION TO GOOD SUCESS

This is not your ordinary book about success. In fact, it's quite the contrary. Success, for many, has a myriad of meanings. Oftentimes, who you are and what you believe determines how you define success. While success can be defined in many different ways, it's important to note that success is much too important to *not* be properly defined. This word can't be left for open interpretation. We have to be intentional and clear on the definition of success for our lives.

Defining Success

In my first book, *Greatness Unleashed: Inspire. Inform. Instruct. Impact.* I redefine the term greatness. In this book, I'll redefine success, causing you to see the word differently than how it is commonly viewed. Success is most often defined as reaching a goal or aim. However, it's important to note that not all goals or aims are *good*. In fact, success, as it is most commonly defined, is not exactly *good success*. This doesn't mean that conventional success is bad; however, it normally only benefits the one who is considered successful. *Good success*, on the other hand, expands far beyond personal gain. So, how do you obtain good success?

In the first chapter of Joshua in the Bible, you find the answer to this question. After succeeding Moses as the leader of God's people, Joshua had some real concerns. He was young, he was nervous and he missed his former leader, Moses. However, God reminds him in Joshua 1:8 that success is available to him if he continues to follow God's Word.

God says to Joshua, *"This Book of the Law shall not depart from your mouth, but you shall meditate on it day and night, so that you may be careful to do according to all that is written in it. For then you will make your way prosperous, and then you will have good success.*

I want to draw your attention to the verbiage God uses by saying, *"good success"*. If all success was the same, there would be no need for God to use the phrase, *"good success."* This confirms that all success is not *good*. Good success can only come by fulfilling God's plan for your life—by reaching the goals that God has for your life. In addition, good success seeks to help others and is void of selfish pursuits. Good success requires a God-first mentality. This mentality says, "Accomplishing God's will for my life is most important." Furthermore, following the plan that God outlines for your life is what will ultimately lead you to good success.

God has a plan for us all. Since His plans for us vary, so will our assignments. However, any plan that God has for you will always have in mind the wellbeing of His creation. God desires that all people experience His salvation and goodness. Therefore, it is imperative that you seek God for understanding and clarity as to how He wants you to fulfill this desire. Furthermore, we must follow His Word. God's Word will ultimately be the blueprint that will assist us in reaching good success.

Like Joshua, we may be fearful at times. We may even have some reluctance about carrying out the assignment that God has set before us. But if we will follow God's plan for our lives, we will not only prosper, but have good success. Don't just settle for any kind of success. Pursue *good success*.

The Blueprint of Good Success

In trying to understand the concept of good success, I've discovered that there is a distinct blueprint that produces this success. The blueprint of good success is found within the spelling of the word *success*. Each letter of the word helps us better understand God's blueprint for successful living. With each letter, S-U-C-C-E-S-S, we will understand what it means to truly have good success. In addition, we will extract truths from the experiences of Joshua as told in the Bible. Finally, we will conclude this book with principles that will help you inspire and impact others to have good success as well.

By discovering these principles, you will understand success in a much deeper way. It is my goal that you will view success beyond the societal norms of acquiring money and fame—beyond educational accolades and professional accomplishments. Don't get me wrong! These things have their place. In fact, these things can be great and even play a vital role in your good success. But above all, we want to seek to please God. We want to aim to fulfill His plans for our lives. We want godly success. That's the epitome of good success.

By the end of this book, you will understand that good success is what I like to call God success. This success is defined and outlined by God himself. This kind of success is not predicated upon what people define as success. Good success is rooted in godly principles and obedience to those principles. Moreover, you will discover that good success is available to any of us. We only need to be willing and obedient to fulfilling God's plan for our lives. Once we grab hold to this concept, we will, without a doubt, experience good success.

By the end of this book, you will understand that good success is what I like to call God success. This success is defined and outlined by God himself. This kind of success is not predicated upon what people define as success. Good success is rooted in godly principles and obedience to those principles. Moreover, you will discover that good success is available to any of us. We only need to be willing and obedient to fulfilling God's plan for our lives. Once we grab hold to this concept, we will, without a doubt, experience good success.

GOOD SUCCESS REQUIRES A GOD-FIRST MENTALITY.

#GOODSUCCESSBOOK

Chapter One

THE BLUEPRINT

Every clever invention starts with an idea. Inventions such as the automobile, the cell phone and the computer all started out as mere ideas. However, all of the aforementioned things are synonymous because they offer ease to the lives of people worldwide. People benefit more from these tools because, instead of just remaining an idea, the inventor made the idea into tangible. Good success is very much the same way. People will best appreciate the idea of good success when it becomes tangible—when it becomes real.

But let's not put the cart before the horse. Before one can achieve good success, you must identify what it looks like. You must follow the blueprint.

Is your idea of success being rich? Perhaps you see someone as successful if they are well-educated. Maybe you base your definition of success on the amount of influence a person has. However, these things don't necessarily amount to good success. *Good success* only comes as a result of fulfilling your God-given purpose, and fulfilling your God-given purpose can only come as a result of being obedient to Him.

Good success won't always equate to riches and wealth. Having good success won't always lead to one being recognized and acclaimed for his or her efforts. Being credentialed and decorated with educational accolades doesn't guarantee good success either. While these things certainly can play a part in good success, it is truly measured by following the plan of God for your life. Good success requires that we honor God and reverence Him as the head of our lives. We must seek Him for direction in order to be successful. Moreover, good success endeavors to make an impact through the call of God. You may have plenty of wealth. You may be very educated and even very well-known. But that doesn't mean that you're making an impact.

As we explore this concept of good success, remember the big picture principles:

- Obedience to God
- Honoring and reverencing God
- And impacting lives

At the root of good success is serving God, as well as serving others. Everything you do should be an act of service.

It's Better to Obey

Have you ever accomplished something and afterward, what you accomplished was not fully esteemed as *good*? While you may have celebrated, somehow others were still displeased with your accomplishment. There have been times in my life when I thought my actions were good, but despite my good intentions, my actions weren't received well by those I wanted to impress most.

It's absolutely possible to do something you deem as good, but it not benefit your life and the progress thereof. Just because something is right doesn't mean it is *good*. The Bible puts it this way, *"I am allowed to do anything"*--but not *everything is good....You say, "I am allowed to do anything"--but not everything is beneficial* (1 Corinthians 10:23 NLT).

The biblical story of King Saul teaches us a valuable lesson as it relates to good success. King Saul proved that one can *believe* that he or she has succeeded, but yet still lack good success. This is important to understand because the goal in this life is not just to be successful—it's to have good success.

God gave Saul an assignment shortly after he was appointed king. The details of this assignment can be found in 1 Samuel 15. In short, God told Saul to go in and destroy the Amalekites for their wicked acts committed toward God's people in times past. God told Saul to wipe them out completely, leaving nothing behind. However, Saul decided to spare the life of the king of the Amalekites. In addition, Saul kept certain possessions he deemed as valuable.

After doing what he thought was right, Saul was greeted by Samuel, one of God's messengers. Saul greeted Samuel with eagerness and happiness, and said to him, "I have done as God has instructed." But upon further analysis, Samuel discovered that Saul was only partially obedient to God. He did destroy the Amalekites, but not in entirety as God instructed him. Saul kept possessions that he shouldn't have, and the life of their king was not to be spared. Samuel warned Saul that obedience is what God requires and that without obedience to God, our acts are futile—no matter how well our intentions.

As a result of his partial obedience, Saul was rejected by God and would eventually be replaced. Here are a couple of lessons we can glean from this story:

1. *Partial obedience is still disobedience.* Although Saul did *most* of what he was asked, he left some things undone. Therefore, it was what he *didn't do* that caused him to be disobedient. Sometimes, what you do correctly can be completely overshadowed by what you failed to do. Think about the times when a professional basketball player had an overall good game, but at the very end, he or she misses an important shot. Somehow, people lose sight of all the good shots the player made and they focus only on the failure. It's important that as we seek success in our lives, we follow through until the end. Be sure that you are doing everything possible to fulfill all requirements.

We can't afford to be lax. We must be obedient and submitted to God's complete plan. We must submit ourselves to God as a child does to his or her parent. A good parent only wants the best for their child. Therefore, they develop strategic guidelines to ensure their children experience nothing but the best. God's plan is always the best plan, and there is always a greater purpose linked to His plan. More importantly, when we fulfill God's plans for our lives, we will have satisfaction, peace and joy.

> 2. *God defines good success.* This is an inescapable truth that cannot be reiterated enough. The *only* way to experience good success is by adhering to God's standards for success. As Saul learned, success cannot be simply something that we assume to be good. It must be intentional. It requires full commitment to God and His will. In order to be committed to His will, you must be attentive to hear the instructions that God outlines for your life and purpose. Because everyone has a unique, God-given assignment, it is imperative that you lend your ear to hear what God requires specifically of you.

If you're not careful, you'll end up like Saul--believing that you have done well when you haven't. When we keep God's definition of success in the forefront of our pursuits, we will avoid the pitfalls that attempt to ensnare us with bad success. Avoid falling victim to your thoughts and lean on God for direction. When we acknowledge Him in all of our ways, He will not only direct our paths, but He will lead us in the way of prosperity, fulfillment and ultimately, good success.

Results of Good Success

Good success yields good fruit. Unlike Saul in our previous story, God will be pleased with you. Good success doesn't leave one feeling regret, loss or even remorse. While it is possible to feel positive emotions without having good success, as Saul did initially, your main focus should be to please God. You know God is pleased when your actions line up with His Word. One quote says, "It's not the will of God if it goes against the Word of God." This is why God tells Joshua to meditate on the Word day and night, and to observe all that is in the Word. By meditating on His Word, we know what pleases God and can follow this understanding with the corresponding actions.

Furthermore, good success brings us, and others, closer to God. If you continue to read the story of Joshua, you'll see how Joshua's reverence of God garnered his success. But more importantly, you'll see His relationship with God grow, which caused those he was leading to grow in relationship with God as well. In addition, because of Joshua's commitment to God, he and the children of Israel were able to reap the rewards that were made available to them. For example, the children of Israel were able to occupy the land that God promised the people under the leadership of Joshua. This, unfortunately, was something they were unable to do while under Moses' leadership.

Good success allows you to reap the benefits of God and receive all God has promised you. Good success satisfies and fills the voids in our lives. The results are prominent. When you experience good success in any area of your life, it is evident that God is with you. This evidence isn't always experienced in material manifestation. But above all, good success brings about godly prosperity—prosperity that produces joy and peace despite one's current circumstances. Good success ensures that all of our needs are met. Above all, it means God is pleased with your life. When God is pleased, everything else is a bonus.

We must be honest about where we fall short and be intentional in making sure we are pleasing to God. Good success is available to us all. While many of us are still in pursuit of experiencing good success in all areas of our lives, it's okay if there are still areas that are lacking. However, it's not okay to do nothing about it. Therefore, embrace the principles in this book and work toward experiencing the God-type of success in all areas of your life.

IT'S NOT THE WILL OF GOD IF IT GOES AGAINST THE WORD OF GOD.

GOD PROVIDES THE BLUEPRINT FOR GOOD SUCCESS.
#GOODSUCCESSBOOK

Chapter Two

THE FIRST "S" – STRENGTH

As we follow God's blueprint for good success, we will discover how each letter of the word "success" provides a clear outline for achieving Godly success. The first "s" in the word success deals with strength. Ephesians 6:10 says, *Be strong in the Lord and in the power of his might.* Furthermore, Philippians 4:13 (NKJV) says, *"I can do all things through Christ who strengthens me."* These scriptures reveal that all things are possible through God's strength. At the foundation of good success is total reliance on God to strengthen you and see you through. There is only so much we can do by merit of our strength. We need God to make us strong.

God's strength, if we allow it, enables us to withstand all of the battles we will face in our pursuit of good success. Through His strength, we cannot fail and we always end up in the winning side.

In Ephesians 6, we are reminded to be strong in the Lord. In verses 13 -17, the Word of God tells us how to be strong, which is through the armor of God. These verses define the helmet of salvation, the breastplate of righteousness and the shield of faith. These passages also address having our feet covered with the gospel of peace and the sword of the Spirit, which is the Word of God. By examining each piece of the armor, I've discovered how these pieces aid us in becoming successful.

- *The Belt of Truth:* In biblical times, soldiers' apparel looked like long robes. I'm not trying to be funny; it's just my best description of their clothing. These garments often flowed down all the way to their ankles. As you can imagine, it would be mighty difficult to properly engage in battle with such restrictive clothing. Therefore, they tied belts around their waists in order to tuck in a great portion of their garments. This allowed for much freer movements

and allowed the soldiers to be more effective in battle.

Paul, the writer of Ephesians, refers to this belt as truth. Why? Because lies are a hindrance. They are restrictive—both to those who lie and even for those who are lied on. The only thing that can free you for battle is truth. As Jesus said, *"You shall know the truth, and the truth shall make you free"* (John 8:32).

Regardless of the amount of lies in the world, in order to have good success, you're going to need truth. Don't stumble over the lies of the enemy. Rather, allow God's Word to guide you into truth. Let it be the light for your pathway—keeping you on the road to success.

- *The Breastplate of Righteousness:* In battle, the breastplate protected the upper body. From a spiritual and success viewpoint, the breastplate protects our hearts. Proverbs 4:23 (NLT) says, *Guard your heart above all else, for it determines the course of your life.*

The condition of your heart determines the quality of your life. Your actions are a mere reflection of what's in your heart. Therefore, if we are going to have a pleasant life, we must fill our hearts with pleasantries. We must guard our hearts against bitterness, resentment, anger and jealousy. Our hearts must be honest and loving, unbiased and true. Allow righteousness to fill your heart. In doing so, you will have a defense for the wickedness you are sure to face.

- *Feet Covered & Ready for Battle:* Ephesians 6:15 (ASV) says, *"Having shod your feet with the preparation of the gospel of peace."* This verse reveals many things to us. One simple way to look at this verse is to refer to your feet being covered by shoes. In battle, shoes were very important, particularly during biblical war times. Often, soldiers had spiked shoes that were designed to help a soldier stand his ground. Like these soldiers, in order to have good success, we must be ready to stand our ground. You will have opposition, but those who will be successful are those who won't be moved.

In addition, you will be able to stand firm in your declaration of faith. For the believers, standing firm means to declare the Good News of Christ. For those who seek good success, one must echo God's Word. Despite all the naysayers, we must still declare the truth. In doing so, we will find peace and satisfaction.

- *The Shield of Faith:* Hebrews 11:6 says, *Without faith it is impossible to please God.* It's impossible to have good success without pleasing God. Good success is *God success*. Therefore, if faith pleases God, we need faith in order to be successful.

Doubt is ever present in this world. In fact, one of the toughest fights we will ever ensue is the fight of faith. If the enemy can get you to doubt, you have already lost the battle. The shield of faith is a necessary piece of armor. Moreover, the shield of faith guards our spirits from the onslaught of evil attacks. With this shield, we are able to find refuge from the fiery darts of the wicked. We avoid the darts of fear, worry, stress and depression. The shield of faith helps us maintain courage, peace, and joy, even while in battle.

- *The Helmet of Salvation:* A helmet's main objective is to protect the head. In battle, it is imperative that you keep your head covered and safe from harm. In the battle for success, you need to cover your mind. Protect your mind from negativity, doubt, temptation and evil. Any helmet won't do. We need the helmet of salvation.

We need salvation for our souls. In addition, we need salvation for our minds. Salvation equates to freedom and deliverance. In order to have good success, our minds need to be free from everything that can be a hindrance. Our minds must be clear and focused on how we can fulfill our God-given assignments.

It's imperative that we protect our minds. Furthermore, we need to make sure we feed our minds with things that are conducive to success. A dirty, cluttered mind is just as dangerous as an exposed head in battle. Our mind is a battlefield. A sound mind, a protected mind is essential to us winning the battle.

- *The Sword of the Spirit:* Jesus said in John 6:63, *"The words that I speak unto you, they are spirit, and they are life."* The sword of the Spirit is God's Word. His Word brings life, truth and understanding. Despite death and bad successes that try to confront us, the Word of God causes us to maintain life. Hebrews 4:12 (NKJV) says, *The word of God is living and powerful, and sharper than any two-edged sword.*

In this entire passage where the armor of God is described, the only weapon mentioned is God's Word. With this living and powerful weapon, we have all that we need to combat the enemies of our success. His word is truth and righteousness. God's Word is salvation. His Word is faith and His Word is life.

God's Word is the preeminent tool that we need to achieve good success. As echoed in Joshua, it is not to depart out of our mouths, and we are to meditate on it day and night. Moreover, we are to follow the Word of God so that our paths will be prosperous, leading us to good success.

You're Equipped for the Battle

With strength from God, we have all we need to accomplish good success. However, we often find ourselves in doubt or despair. We sometimes forget that God makes strength available to us. When we fail to utilize the strength made available to us, we remain idle and unsuccessful. It's important that you resolve in your mind that you are enough, and you have what it takes to be successful. No matter how great the obstacles are in your life, you can win.

We never have to doubt that we have the ability to complete the tasks before us. I like to remind myself, and others, that if God calls you to something, He has already equipped you to complete the task. He has equipped you for battle. Not only that, He has already given you the victory. We are more than conquers through Him (Romans 8:37). If you ever feel weak, remember that you can do all things through Christ, who strengthens you. Although you may be weak, He is strong. Through your trust and faith in God, He will reveal His strength.

One of my favorite examples of this is when God reveals His strength to the Apostle Paul in his moment of weakness. After praying to God three times to have an issue removed from his life, God revealed to Paul that His grace is all that Paul needed for this issue. Paul, by receiving God's grace and favor, found strength to be able to rejoice, despite his circumstances. Here's a major key that we must always remember: God will never place in you a situation that you cannot handle. As the famous quote says, "God will not put more on you than you can bear." When you recognize this, like Paul, you will be able to stay consistent and steadfast in your faith.

Paul discovered that in his weakness, God's strength is revealed. Paul discovered that He was equipped to handle his battles. Like Paul, exchange your weakness for God's strength. Exchange your fears for His faith. Exchange your idea of success for God's idea of success. You have all you need in Him.

Our strength comes solely from God. It is, *In Him that we live, we move and have our being* (Acts 17:28). Without Him, we could do nothing. Therefore, depend on God today. He has equipped and enabled you for good success. By His strength, you will achieve it.

It Gets Better

Now before I get ahead of myself, let me say that 'better' doesn't always mean easy. Consider the old saying, "Life doesn't get easier; you simply get stronger." When you get stronger, things get better.

I remember training in the weight room as a young man in high school. One of my goals was to constantly increase my weight repetitions. I wanted to become stronger. I wanted to get better. I even joined others in the goal of beating our max reps. After lifting our heaviest weight possible, we added more pounds to see if we could lift that. This was called a "max." Lifting the max weight was never easy. However, our chances were greatly increased depending on how strong we were at the time. The only way to become stronger is by continually exercising the muscles you need to achieve your goals.

Those type of weight-lifting days are behind me, as I no longer lift for sport. But I learned something valuable through those experiences – with strength things get better. Through continual exercise, I grew stronger; therefore, I was able to achieve more. Thus, I was able to experience better results. The stronger you are, the better you become. The more of God's strength you use, the better your life will be.

It is vital for us to continue to exercise and strengthen our relationship with Him. By increasing our "reps" in His Word, constantly increasing our prayer reps, and being clothed in the proper garments (Armor of God), our exercise becomes easier. By listening to God's instruction, like an athlete to a coach, we become better suited to achieve good success. Yes, the battles that we face may be difficult at times. But as we grow in God's strength, things will get better.

GOD WILL NEVER PLACE IN YOU A SITUATION THAT YOU CANNOT HANDLE.
#GOODSUCCESSBOOK

Chapter Three

"U" – UNITY

John Dickinson said, "United we stand, divided we fall." This quote is a reflection of the idea that unity breeds strength, while division produces failure. In my first book, I talk about the power of relationships. We all need each other to be successful. No one can be successful by their own efforts. Moreover, good success requires the assistance of someone else to accomplish the set goal.

Someone will contribute to your success in one way or another. Take this book for example. Many people played a part in the production of this book. Someone designed the cover and the interior of the book. An editor helped perfect the spelling and grammar. Someone had to print the book. Alone, I am unable to accomplish all these things. I utilize platforms built by others to produce and promote my book. Lastly, but maybe more importantly, I need readers to help spread this message. If no one ever reads this book, this message will never be heard. We all need the contributions of others to experience success.

No man is an island unto himself. No one was created by himself, for himself, for the betterment of himself alone. Therefore, it is vital that we join with others who can assist us in becoming successful. An athlete depends on a team. A speaker requires an audience. To create a family, you need someone to help make this possible. Unity makes the road less traveled a little easier to travel. Unity provides a little more assurance that you can indeed have good success.

The Power of Unity

Ecclesiastes 4:9 (ASV) says, *Two are better than one, because they have a good reward for their labor.* We can accomplish more together than we can alone. There is indeed power in numbers. The following verses go on to explain that if one were to fall and is alone, they all will have major problems. However, if you fall and you have someone with you, that person can lift you up and in aid you in time of trouble. Verse 12 highlights how our enemies can prevail against us much easier if we stand alone. But if we have another with us, we will be able to withstand our enemy. In addition, the writer reveals to us that a three-fold cord is not easily broken.

One revelation I received regarding the three-fold cord is that it represents *loyalty, trust* and *fellowship*. Together, these three components produce unity. With love, trust and fellowship, it is very difficult, impossible even, for you to fail.

- *Loyalty:* There is nothing like having someone who is with you through the thick and thin. This person is someone who is committed to you and your success. They are faithful and loving. Gifts, talents and resources are all good. But, having a multitude of people around can be helpful, as well. However, if you have all of these things without *loyal* people, it can be tremendously difficult to have good success.

It is also vital that you are loyal—loyal to others and loyal to God. In fact, your loyalty to God will produce compassion that will empower you to be faithful to others. Furthermore, when we follow the example of Christ, we see a man who is loyal to His friends and this world. He is loyal in seeing that we experienced God's power. He is loyal in showing us the way that leads to life and that more abundantly. He was loyal in giving His life for us. Jesus showed the ultimate love and loyalty by laying down His life for us. This was not only for His benefit, but for the benefit of all mankind. Let Christ be your example of loyalty. Your loyalty, as well as the loyalty of those whom you unite with, should mirror Christ's loyalty.

- *Trust:* Trust represents confidence and security. As a woman trusts her husband to protect and provide for the family, we must have confidence in those who are with us on our success journey. When you have the God-type of success at the forefront of your mind, you are intentional in linking up with people who you can trust, people that you know you can depend on. Like loyalty, you should be able to trust anyone that you're connected to. But, more importantly, you should commit to being trustworthy, as well. Here's a simple truth: You will never attract trustworthy people if *you* can't be trusted.

- *Fellowship:* As we connect with others, it's imperative that we have comradery. Fellowship allows deeper insight into the thoughts, feelings, strengths and weaknesses of those you have relationships with.

In football, it is very common during team camps and travels for the quarterback to room with the wide receiver. The quarterback's job is to get the ball to the wide receiver on the field. Therefore, to further understand his teammate, he spends as much time as possible with the guy he's hoping to pass the to. This increases the chances of the team being successful.

In this game of life, we have to gain knowledge about those whom we will partner or play with. If we are going to have unity, we need fellowship in order to strengthen our bonds.

Uniting with the Vision

One critical element of unity is mutual understanding and agreement of the goal or task at hand. It is impossible for people to stand in agreement without a clear understanding of what they're attempting to accomplish. If you hope to have good success, the vision has to be clear. Moreover, there must be unity with the vision. For example, an employee can't have good success on the job if he or she refuses to align with the vision of the company. A marriage cannot be

successful if the husband and wife are continually divided. Neither can a team win without the unified efforts of all of those involved. This is why Jesus says in Matthew 12:25, *Every kingdom divided against itself is brought to desolation; and every city or house divided against itself shall not stand.* If we are going to stand, we must do so together. Otherwise, we will have division, and this will only produce failure and defeat.

As we endeavor to live the life God has mapped out for us, we must be intentional in forming unions that will be beneficial to our aim. Moreover, we must purpose to fulfill our obligations as outlined by God. Vision for good success comes from God. Therefore, it is vital that you grab hold of what He has envisioned for your life. You can't pursue things contrary to God's plan and still claim to be united with His vision. Unity requires a willingness to follow God's lead. Good success is impossible to achieve without unity.

WE CAN ACCOMPLISH MORE TOGETHER THAN WE CAN ALONE.

#GOODSUCCESSBOOK

VISION FOR GOOD SUCCESS COMES FROM GOD.

#GOODSUCCESSBOOK

Chapter Four

THE FIRST "C" – COURAGE

There's a quote by Zig Ziglar, which says, "Fear is false evidence appearing real." This is one of my favorite quotes, and I constantly rehearse these words during challenging moments. However, I once believed this quote to mean that fear is not real, or that fear is just a figment of my imagination. I soon learned I was wrong. Fear is certainly real. However, the outcomes, the evidence that fear presents to you does not have to be real. Fear begins in our minds, and it rests in our actions, often impeding our progress. Therefore, if you can condition your mind to believe in your abilities and the gifts that God has given you, you will recognize that fear has no real power. I am not suggesting that you will never have reservations when following God's blueprint for success. In fact, when building anything, there are always concerns, doubts and even fears. However, acknowledge that they exist, and use God's Word to combat these obstacles.

First Timothy 1:7 says, *God has not given us the spirit of fear....* Fear doesn't come from God. Therefore, if you are experiencing fear, realize that God is not in it. God wants us to operate from faith. Faith is our shield, our strength to combat the darts of fear that will oppose us. Fear might be present, but remember what God has spoken regarding your good success. Operate from faith in His words, and you will defeat fear. Feel the fear, and do it anyway. Yes, you may feel fear when you pursue good success, but pursue it anyway. You may feel as if you are unable to accomplish the tasks that God has placed before you, but do it anyway. Don't allow fear to hinder you. Be fearless. The more you operate in faith, the less you will fear.

Hebrews 11:1 says, *Faith is the substance of things hoped, the evidence of things not seen.* Your faith produces hope. Your faith will provide the evidence to continue to seek what you cannot see. Think about in the context of a crime scene. When investigators are trying to determine who committed a crime, they look for evidence.

FEAR BEGINS IN OUR MINDS, AND IT RESTS IN OUR ACTION.

#GOODSUCCESSBOOK

The evidence points them in the direction of the one(s) who committed the crime. Faith is the same way. It provides the direction to help you navigate through the issues in your life. Faith provides the evidence for what you are hoping to accomplish. On the other hand, fear provides false evidence and if you follow it, that evidence will get you off course. Stay the course and keep your confidence in God. Rehearse the promises of God. Remind yourself that He is the same God today that He was in times past. If He blessed in times past, He'll do it again.

Be Strong and Courageous

One of the things that made Joshua such an effective leader was his ability to overcome fear. Joshua constantly reminded himself of God's promises and His goodness. However, this wasn't always the case for Joshua. He, too, had times where he experienced fear and doubt. After the death of Moses, Joshua was in a place of uncertainty and fear. For years, he followed and supported Moses as he led the people of God toward their promise. Joshua would have given his very life for Moses. When Moses died, it left a major void in Joshua's heart. Moreover, Joshua was thrust into a position that, for many, would be overwhelming. I believe Joshua early on felt that pressure and was unsure of his ability to lead the people forward.

These feelings of hesitation and doubt are common for many of us. There are some opportunities presented to us that we may believe are too much to handle. However, we have to be reminded that God is with us, and that we only need to be courageous. We can be courageous, not because we are great alone, but because of who stands with us. Romans 8:31 reminds us, *If God be for us, who can be against us?* As believers of God in Jesus Christ, we can take solace in the fact that God with us is more than any enemy against us.

God says to Joshua in Joshua 1:6-7, *"Be strong and of a good courage…Only be thou strong and very courageous….* God explains to Joshua that he has no need to be afraid and that victory and success is eminent. We have to understand that as God calls us to an assignment, He makes available the way for us to be successful in that assignment. Like Joshua, we only need to be strong and courageous in God. This will ensure good success.

As mentioned in the second chapter, we are to, *Be strong in the Lord….* (Ephesians 6:10). Without Him, our strength is futile and will not endure. Therefore, in telling Joshua to be strong and courageous, God further outlines how this is made possible. The first thing God does is remind Joshua of the promise that He made to Moses. As promised to Moses, the children of Israel would one day become inhabitants of the land promised to them. The promise of God did not end with Moses. Often we think that if we're not the ones to accomplish a task, it can't be done. Sometimes, God uses us to set someone else up for good success. Although, Moses did not physically see the Promised Land himself, without his contributions, Joshua wouldn't have been able to be successful as a leader. Never discount your efforts today because someone will benefit from them tomorrow.

Because God made a promise to Moses, Joshua could rest in the fact that God would finish the work He started. Like Joshua, we, too, can rest in the promises of God. For, *God is not a man that He should lie...* (Numbers 23:19). If God said it, that settles it, and we can find strength in His promises.

Joshua had to remain strong and courageous because he had to stay committed to God's Word. It can indeed be challenging to follow God's Word, particularly when there is the temptation to do the opposite. The world is a place that can weaken us in our pursuits of good success if we are not diligent to the Word of God. Oddly enough, our strength comes from continued obedience and acknowledgement of His Word. This is why God tells Joshua to turn *not* from the Word so that he would be prosperous wherever he went. In being attentive to God's instructions, you will prosper wherever He leads you.

Stay Committed

During his transition, Joshua really didn't have much time to mourn the death of Moses, nor did he have the time to dwell on his inabilities. Joshua had to remain committed to the work that preceded him. Joshua couldn't afford to give up and quit on his assignment. Much like Joshua, we all have assignments that we must fulfill in this life. In order to satisfy the requirements of our life's tasks, we must stay committed to the call. Galatians 6:9 says, *Let us not be weary in well doing: for in due season we shall reap, if we faint not.* Any good pursuit will be faced with challenges and obstacles. Therefore, it is imperative that we learn the importance of commitment. Without commitment to the task, you are sure to quit when tough times come.

One of my favorite definitions for commitment is, "the ability to stick to what you said you were going to do, long after the initial excitement has left you." At the initial onset of a goal, many people are enthused and excited about accomplishing their goals. Our excitement is great and it is needed to help us get started. However, we will need more than excitement to maintain our consistency in pursuing our goals. With all of this talk about good success, it should be noted that there are many enemies to good success. Not everyone wants you to experience godly success. The road to good success, while paved with good intentions, is not an easy one.

I never want to mislead anyone; therefore, I want you to know that good success requires work. However, our work can be less complex when we are committed to God. Proverbs 16:3 NLT says, *Commit your actions to the Lord, and your plans will succeed.* When you are committed to God, He will *cause* you to be successful. Commit to God and He will commit to your success. Good success follows those who are committed to Him.

Psalm 37:4 reminds us to delight ourselves in the Lord, and He will give us the desires of our hearts. Commitment to God positions us to receive from God what's in our hearts because our hearts are focused on pleasing Him. When our hearts are committed to the things of God, we will only pursue good things and have godly desires. God doesn't have an issue blessing us. Your commitment to God will ensure that God will act in accordance to your benefit. Psalm 37:5 says, *Commit your way to the LORD; trust in him, and he will act.* When we are committed to God, He moves on our behalf, making the way possible for us to have good success.

If we are somehow not experiencing the good success that God has made available to us, we must ask ourselves the questions: *Have I committed myself to God like I should? Have I committed my plans to His, or am I following my own desires?* Allow God to conform your will to His. He created us and knows what we need to be successful.

Uncompromising

Along with commitment, in order to embrace and exhibit courage, you must be uncompromising. There is a story in the Bible that surrounds three young men in the third chapter of Daniel. This story showcases the uncompromising dedication that these young men had to God. Their allegiance to God was strong—it was unbreakable.

At the time, the king put a law into effect that required everyone to worship a statue. This law was contrary to the beliefs of the three young men: Shadrach, Meshach and Abednego. Constrained by their faith, they refused to follow the custom of worshipping another God. The impending

punishment was death if they didn't comply. Yet, they refused. Shadrach, Meshach and Abednego were eventually placed into a furnace, as mandated by the king, because they refused to worship the golden statue. However, much to the king's amazement, as well as the other witnesses, the three young men were not consumed. The fire did not harm them. God had indeed protected them from the effects of the fire.

For many of us, we have been and will continue to be placed in positions where we will be pressed to compromise our faith. This world we presently live in is constantly attacking the values that we hold dear. In order to maintain good success, we have to see the consequences of the proverbial fire, but remain uncompromising to God's truth. The heat from the fire may intensify in your life. But if you simply hold fast to God's Word, the fire will not harm you.

The thing I love about Shadrach, Meshach and Abednego is that they remained respectful and dignified. They didn't allow the pressures of society to cause them to act out of character, and neither can we. We can be uncompromising, and respectful and loving at the same time. All too often we witness people with strong beliefs that are intolerant of others. You can embrace your truth without being disrespectful of someone else's beliefs. You don't have to agree with someone to love and respect them. The mark of a true follower of Christ is love; by this shall all men know that we are His disciples. Our love will have the biggest impact on changing the world.

Good success means that you operate from a set of values that are non-negotiable because the ultimate goal is to honor God. People who experience good success don't simply practice their faith; they live their faith. They embody faith. Our faith is what causes us to triumph. You cannot have good success if you conform to the status quo and compromise. Be strong. Be bold. Be godly. Be successful.

COMMIT TO GOD AND HE WILL COMMIT TO YOUR SUCCESS.

#GOODSUCCESSBOOK

Chapter Five

THE SECOND "C"- CONTENTMENT

Contentment is somewhat of a foreign concept in the realm of traditional success. When you view success through the definition of society, there seems to be a never-ending pursuit of goals. Seldom is one satisfied with his or her level of success. Many people say, "I'm addicted to success," or, "I won't quit until I'm on top." In many regards, this behavior rarely leads to satisfaction and contentment. Contentment comes from the word *content,* which means to be pleased and satisfied; not needing more. *Contentment* is the state of being pleased and satisfied.

When pursuing *good success,* contentment is necessary. In fact, God's Word teaches that contentment, along with godliness, is great gain. Though this is an odd concept indeed for many, contentment settles you and allows you to be free to pursue what God desires for your life. Contentment brings about a stillness and sensitivity to the voice of God that allows you to follow the plan of success that He outlines for you. In order to understand this concept further, let's visit one of the profound teachings of Jesus found in Matthew 6.

A Kingdom First Mentality

Matthew 6:33 says, *"Seek the Kingdom of God above all else, and live righteously, and He will give you everything you need."* These words spoken by Christ reminds us that when our attention is focused in the right direction, we will find fulfillment and satisfaction. In the following verses, Jesus implores us to focus solely on today and not worry about what tomorrow may bring. Jesus recognizes that today brings its own set of issues that requires our undivided attention in order to excel. When we are overly eager for material gain and lack contentment, we will miss the valuable lessons that each day tries to teach us.

Each day equips us with the necessary tools to succeed the next day and the day after. If we neglect to appreciate the present, we enter into the future unprepared. This causes frustration, regret and ultimately, a delay in our good success.

Be content with where God has you. Be content with today's assignment, and focus solely on God's agenda. In doing so, everything you need will be provided to you. We have to trust that God will supply all of our needs according to His riches in glory, as promised in Philippians 4:19. Like Paul says, *"My dear brothers and sisters, stand firm. Let nothing move you. Always give yourselves fully to the work of the Lord, because you know that your labor in the Lord is not in vain"* (1 Corinthians 15:58 NIV). When you seek God first, and commit to working for Him, you will be rewarded. Your labor and efforts will not go unnoticed. Therefore, be content. Be patient, and be faithful to God.

Of course, I am not suggesting that you don't set goals or endeavor to accomplish great things. However, our efforts and goals are to be filtered through what God deems successful. Contentment simply means pursuing what pleases God and avoiding that which is unsatisfactory to Him. It doesn't mean that we are to be idle. It simply means that our intentions are to please Him above all else, seeking to fulfill your godly assignment first.

Embrace Your Purpose

Contentment allows you to embrace who God created you to be and the purpose for which He created you. Since your purpose and good success are intertwined, it's mandatory to embrace your purpose.

CONTENTMENT SIMPLY MEANS PURSUING WHAT PLEASES GOD AND AVOIDING THAT WHICH IS UNSATISFACTORY TO HIM.

#GOODSUCCESSBOOK

God created us all with a purpose. When we pursue that purpose, we are on the road to good success. Furthermore, God has made it possible for us to reach this goal through His Word and by the gifts and strengths He's placed within us. The Word of God is a great enabler. It gives us the power to activate the abilities God has placed within us. Through this power God's plan is easily fulfilled.

Joshua was a skilled warrior, a master strategist and a man of boldness. These attributes allowed Joshua to not only have good success, but he was also able to lay the foundation for others to do the same. As Joshua used his strengths to fulfill his purpose, he was able to make an impact by leading many in the way of God.

In everything you do, remember that the end goal is to impact lives. Therefore, when pursuing your passions, be certain that lives are sincerely impacted in your pursuits. Godly success requires you to be unselfish. Your passions can't be self-centered. If you help others obtain success, you, too, will obtain success. Don't ever think that by helping others you are somehow neglecting yourself. Quite the contrary happens. You better position yourself for greatness and success when you aid others into great success. What you make happen for someone else, God makes happen for you. In other words, you reap what you sow. If you sow good things, you will reap good things. Therefore, embrace your purpose and embrace the responsibility of impacting lives.

Contentment Requires Good Character

Who you are when no one is watching is the most commonly used definition for character. This definition has much validity since the truth is that no individual is able to watch you 24 hours a day, seven days a week. However, God is always watching. Therefore, you can practice good character when you realize that although no human being is always present, God is ever present. Since our desire is to attain godly success, we should maintain good character.

Good character helps us maintain consistency and commitment to the goals at hand. Therefore, even when you're tempted with something that doesn't align with your goals and purpose, your character will remind you that it's not worth the compromise. It is fairly easy to become distracted and lose sight of your purpose if you have poor character. People of poor character chase every opportunity that looks good. But just because it seems good doesn't mean it's good. Good character will arrest your desires and keep them focused on what's truly good for you. Good character is the foundation upon which contentment can stand strong, causing you to continue in your pursuit to please God.

Many people allow their present circumstances and desire for material wealth to hinder their progress toward good success. When people are tempted to fail in their character, it sways them toward ungodly pursuits. This is why people resort to things like selling drugs, prostitution and theft. People who are distracted only by what they don't have miss the wealth that is wrapped in the gift of contentment. When you lose focus of what God has available for you, your life seems incomplete. Rather than seeing your life as lacking, see it as God preparing you for greater opportunities.

We must be like the Apostle Paul and declare, *"Whatever state I find myself in, I will be content."* Remain consistent, patient and focused, and don't let go of good character. Remember contentment is a Kingdom-first mentality. Those who have a Kingdom-first mentality never come up short. Things may not happen on your timetable. But if you can remain focused and committed, you will eventually have good success.

PEOPLE WHO ARE DISTRACTED ONLY BY WHAT THEY DON'T HAVE MISS THE WEALTH THAT IS WRAPPED IN THE GIFT OF CONTENTMENT.

#GOODSUCCESSBOOK

Chapter Six

"E" – EDUCATION (KNOWLEDGE)

Education simply means to obtain knowledge. Knowledge goes beyond information and requires that information be applied in order to produce education. Knowledge can be summed up in two words: *projected information*. If you break down the word "knowledge", you end up with two words, "know" and "ledge." To know means to be informed. One of the synonyms of ledge it to project. Therefore, if you bridge the two together, you end up with a projection of information. In short, you act out or display what you know.

You've heard before, "When you know better, you do better." Without the proper knowledge, it is difficult, impossible even, to achieve success. In order to experience the God-type of success, it is crucial to have a thorough knowledge of who God is, what He requires, and what He has enabled you to do. With knowledge being so readily available these days, there's no excuse not to have education. Benjamin Franklin said, "We are all born ignorant, but one must work hard to remain stupid." In other words, because knowledge is abundant, it requires more work to remain ignorant.

It's important to understand that education goes beyond academic accomplishments. In fact, some of the most educated persons have never climbed to the ladder of academia. There are some who even contend that, "College isn't for everyone, but education is." As it relates to good success, education can be found in experience as well as a thorough knowledge of God's Word.

One of the reasons why Joshua was able to experience good success is because he saw God work in times past. Joshua was there during the victories that Moses and the children of Israel experienced prior to being under his leadership. Joshua was there when God delivered the people out of Egyptian bondage, and he was there as God sustained them in the wilderness. Through these first-hand experiences,

Joshua's knowledge of who God increased mightily. Another reason Joshua was able to achieve good success was because He remained committed to God's Word.

It is absolutely impossible to have good success without knowledge of God's Word. Since Joshua saw God work on behalf of the people in times of distress, He was able to reverence God by being obedient to His Word.

Many may argue that experience and knowledge isn't necessary to be successful. To a certain degree, this is true. However, conventional success and good success are uniquely different. The great thing about good success is that you only need to be willing to learn. You have to be willing to grow and move beyond your current state. In order to have any type of success, you have to embrace knowledge. You may not like school, and you may not like reading or learning. However, it is sometimes necessary to do things that you don't enjoy in order to position yourself to be successful.

Yes, Joshua experienced the handiwork of God firsthand. However, it didn't start off that way. Joshua didn't begin his life with knowledge. None of us have. But what made Joshua knowledgeable was his willingness to learn. Therefore, he positioned himself in a place where he was able to do so. He became close to Moses, and gleaned as much from him as he possibly could. My suggestion for you is to connect with someone who is where you want to be, and learn as much as you can from that person. You don't necessarily need to be the smartest person in the world to have good success. But you do need to link up with someone who can teach you something about what you're trying to achieve. The smartest person isn't the one who knows everything, but rather the person who recognizes that he doesn't know everything. We can only accomplish so much by ourselves. We need others to help us achieve good success.

The Beginning of Knowledge

Proverbs 1:7 says, *The fear (reverence) of the Lord is the beginning of knowledge.* When you decide to reverence and honor God, you position yourself to receive knowledge. Having reverence for God places you in the posture of humility and submission. Since you are submitted to God, you are able to receive from God the information necessary to be successful. Because of your willingness to learn from God, you become all the wiser.

Proverbs 1:5 says, *Let the wise hear and increase in learning, and the one who understands obtain guidance.* Knowledge gives you wisdom as well as guidance. This is why the writer says, *Order my steps in your word* (Psalm 119:133). God's Word serves as, *"...a lamp unto our feet, a light unto our path* (Psalm 119:105). If we are going to know which direction to take, we must take heed to the Word of God. In addition, as we submit ourselves to God, He will direct us in the way we should go. Furthermore, He will send certain people to aid us in achieving our goals.

Application. Application. Application.

These words are mentioned three times consecutively to place emphasis on the principle of action. There is power in action. Nothing can change as long as you're idle. Change is a direct result of action. As wonderful and euphoric as it to dream, envision, and even recite your goals and desires, nothing will be accomplished without the proper corresponding actions. Therefore, in achieving good success, we have a responsibility to identify the actions necessary to fulfill this goal. This is where application comes into play.

UTILIZE THIS PAGE TO WRITE WHAT YOU PLAN TO APPLY FROM WHAT YOU HAVE LEARNED THUS FAR.

THE SMARTEST PERSON ISN'T THE ONE WHO KNOWS EVERYTHING, BUT RATHER THE PERSON WHO RECOGNIZES THAT HE DOESN'T KNOW EVERYTHING.

#GOODSUCCESSBOOK

"E" – EDUCATION (KNOWLEDGE

Many people know what being a great spouse entails. However, they aren't always aware of how to apply that knowledge. There isn't a shortage of materials and commentary available for anyone desiring to become a great spouse. The problem with some of the information, however, is that many lack the understanding of how to apply this knowledge. No matter your desire, there is a wealth of information available that will make you knowledgeable on how to fulfill your goal. The void comes because many lack the ability to apply the knowledge. Therefore, I have pinpointed four areas that need to be addressed in order to properly apply the knowledge that is so readily available for you:

1. *Identify Your Weaknesses:* Continuing with the example of being a great spouse, being married teaches you a lot. Through much trial and error, you learn what works and what doesn't work for the benefit of your union. One of the biggest hurdles for me in marriage has been accepting that what I might deem to be a strength may in fact be a weakness in my marriage. I only learned this when I realized that I don't know everything.

In order to properly identify your weaknesses, you must first accept that you aren't all-knowing. There's always something that you can learn. You can always improve and better your best. This principle applies whether you're an employee, entrepreneur, speaker, author, mother or father. Regardless of your vocation, responsibilities or position, admit that you have weaknesses. Furthermore, admit that you might not be as strong in an area as you might have initially thought.

Remember, at the foundation of good success is serving God and following His lead. Therefore, good success is less about what you want and more about what God desires. Good success requires you to seek understanding of what God holds in high esteem. Initially, you may see what God desires as difficult to accomplish. This in turn may cause you to recognize that there are areas in your life that need improvement in order to accomplish His will. This humility is the beginning of you gaining the power you need.

Through Joshua's humility, he was able to receive proper instruction from God on how to be successful. Through our humility, God is able to exalt us as He promises in Matthew

23:12. On the contrary, those who lack contrition and exalt themselves will be cut down.

2. *Application Requires the Proper Knowledge:* Knowledge can only equate to power when it is applied. Moreover, in order for knowledge to be applied properly, it needs to match the goal at hand. Football players learn football plays, not basketball plays, in order to win. You study math equations if you want to pass your math quiz. Certainly, you wouldn't teach Dutch to students who are enrolled in a Spanish class. Make sure that the knowledge you seek applies to your goals. What good is information if it isn't useful where you're headed? If we don't acquire the proper knowledge, we won't know which steps to take.

Your godly success hinges upon your ability to learn. While there is a myriad of information that can easily be obtained, it also must be pursued. It's not enough to guess and insinuate. It is your responsibility to learn what you need in order to fulfill your purpose.

3. *Exercise:* Exercise builds strength and stamina. In doing so, those areas of weakness begin to improve. It is imperative that you continue to work to grow stronger. The best teacher for this is experience itself—experience being exercise.

A team never knows how good or bad they are until they are in direct competition with another team. While you may learn a lot in practice, the game is the true test of your knowledge and skill. Your performance helps identify your progress as well as what needs improvement. In addition, you must stay in shape in order to maintain your success, continually improving where you may be weak. This requires constant exercise—constant learning.

Therefore, it's vital that you exercise your brain by increasing in knowledge and exercising your skills by continually testing what you have learned. Keep working and keep improving. There's always room for improvement. Don't neglect the importance of exercise just because you've won a few times. You must stay in shape.

Knowledge puts you in the driver's seat to make the responsible decisions that will produce good success. However, sitting in the driver's seat means nothing if you never drive the car. Having the ability to drive is nothing without applying your driving skills and knowledge. Once you apply what you have learned in the proper areas, good success is more attainable.

The Responsibility of Knowledge

In addition to application, one of the greatest responsibilities of knowledge is to share information with others. It's necessary to share your knowledge with others so they may have an understanding of how they, too, should operate in life. Joshua had to teach others to observe the Word of God. Joshua's assignment was to speak the word continually, constantly reminding the people of God how important it is to bind the Word to their hearts. Today, our responsibilities are no different. With all of the knowledge we will amass in this life, we are to share what we learn with others.

"If you are not living to make someone else's life better, you are wasting your time." Good success not only means that *you* please God, but you also help others please God. Our lives are made up of information passed down to us by someone else. Furthermore, what we lack is often a result of the information and education we lack. If we are going to help others avoid unnecessary pitfalls, we have to be committed to teaching others how to not only avoid these pitfalls, but stay on the path of success.

The Benefits of Knowledge

When properly applied, knowledge can yield a number of benefits. These benefits include, but are not limited to:

- *Empowerment:* To empower is to make strong, to build up. When one is empowered, weaknesses are offset and strengths are magnified. Knowledge replaces your weaknesses with strengths, allowing you to excel in your pursuit of good success.

- *Enlightenment:* What once was dark is now made light. Like a lamp, candle or flashlight in a room without light, knowledge pierces the darkness and helps you navigate properly on the road to success.

- *Endurance:* There are many who fall short of their goals because they lack the information that will keep them going. Many times, you hear someone say, "If I would've known this, I would have done that." Oftentimes, we bow out of the race too early, not realizing that the finish line is closer than we think.

In the book of Numbers, the children of Israel came face to face with the land God promised them. However, due to their finite knowledge and understanding, entering the land was impossible. It was this short-sighted thinking that caused many of them to want to give up and return back to Egypt. However, it was a young Joshua and Caleb that had a proper knowledge of who God was that led them to pursue and overtake the land—land which God had already promised them. Because they had knowledge, they had the wherewithal to endure the necessary process to receive the promise of God. If you want to outlast your tests and obstacles, you must be educated in the proper areas.

- *Enthusiasm/Confidence:* Have you ever taken an exam that you weren't quite prepared for? You felt dread and hesitation. You were worried that you would not fair well because you were not confident in your knowledge. However, when you are confident in what you know, you have a greater excitement and enthusiasm. Sometimes, you can't wait to take the test because you are sure that you will pass.

Life is the same way. In order for us to pass the tests of life, we must be knowledgeable. When you have knowledge, you are able to approach your obstacles with a greater confidence.

In 1 Samuel, Chapter 17, we find the story of an eager, enthusiastic young man by the name of David. In this story, we discover that a group of people called the Philistines assembled themselves to war against the people of God. Unfortunately, the people of God were fearful and reluctant to engage in warfare. However, David was the complete opposite. Instead of cowering in the face of the enemy, David drew on his past knowledge and experiences to remain bold and ready to fight. Because of his past victories with God, David knew that the Philistines would be no different. David remained confident in the fact that if God delivered him before, He would do it again. This knowledge allowed David to be confident that he would be victorious.

Like David, we must pull on past victories to push us past our present obstacles. The fact that you are alive today denotes that God has been with you, and you yet have a purpose. If God has allowed you to excel in times past, you can rest in the fact that He will be with you during present and future hurdles. As we educate ourselves and grow in knowledge, we position ourselves to achieve good success in all areas of our lives. Like an athlete who studies his opponent, we can win if we commit to learning. Never cease to learn. The moment you do so, you cease to grow. Without growth, you forego good success.

Chapter Seven

THE SECOND "S" – SELECTIVE (BE SELECTIVE)

All opportunities aren't *good* opportunities. While pursuing good success, you'll be presented with many opportunities that may appear to be a positive fit for your goals, but may actually be the opposite. Be critical of the things you engage in as you pursue good success. Distractions will come in abundance, but remain focused. Good success requires tunnel vision, relentless focus and immense scrutiny. Some may confuse this approach as conceited, arrogant or standoffish. In short, expect to be misunderstood. It comes with the territory. In being selective, you're not trying to present yourself as superior to others; it just means you simply understand the urgency of fulfilling your purpose.

We have to approach our relationships, business connections and ministry pursuits with the mindset of achieving good success. If it cannot help you maintain and secure good success, it's best that you avoid it. Amos 3:3 (CEB) asks the question, *Will two people walk together unless they have agreed to do so?* In order for there to be unity in any area, there has to be a mutual agreement between all involved parties.

Therefore, as it relates to your purpose and good success, any connections should involve a mutual understanding of goals.

In order to help you stay on the right path, it is important to surround yourself with like-minded people. This doesn't mean that you and those you have relationships with are identical. It simply means that everything and everyone in your life aligns with and respects your godly purpose. It's the idea that Paul presents in 2 Corinthians 6:14 where he cautions believers, *Do not be unequally yoked with unbelievers.* This verse raises contention and debate among many, particularly amongst those who find themselves closely involved with people who aren't like them.

Again, being selective doesn't make you uppity or better than other people, and Paul wasn't suggesting that you act this way.

But there must be an understanding that everyone and all opportunities don't help you acquire good success. Some people aren't evil people, but their understanding and belief of goals may differ from yours. To avoid being swayed away from your righteous pursuits, it's best not to link up with those who believe differently from you. You cannot pursue good success with someone who is not fixed on pursuing good success themselves. This doesn't mean that you can't respect, love and even have communication with those who are different from you. But you must *be selective*.

Learn To Be Ok With Saying, "No"

Growth and change can be challenging, but it's necessary. I'll admit, the idea of saying, "No," or not saying, "Yes" was difficult at first. However, what was more difficult was trying to please everyone who beckoned for my attention. Being a people pleaser is an impossible task. You are certain to disappoint someone. Because you want to please others, you feel guilt and remorse. To avoid this, I'm going to share a technique that I learned from Dr. Eric Thomas, motivational speaker.

Dr. Thomas teaches that you should prioritize goals in your life in four categories: *Not important*, *somewhat*

THE SECOND "S" – SELECTIVE (BE SELECTIVE)

important, very important and emergency. For the sake of this writing, I'll put a different spin on this philosophy and share how this approach relates to good success.

1. *Not Important:* At the onset, this may sound harsh. But, keep an open mind. While something may be important to someone else, it is highly possible that you may not share the same urgency. You shouldn't feel guilty if you don't share the same passion and concerns about something someone else does. Everyone is different. We all process emotions differently, and thought processes vary by person.

When I wrote my first book, I wanted everyone to embrace the book as I did. I soon learned that my expectations were unrealistic. While that book has been well received, and has impacted many lives, there are yet a countless number of people that will never think twice about reading the book, as is the case with any author. To them, it's simply not important. *Not important* frankly means a lack of interest.

Sometimes our feelings are hurt because our ideas aren't received by those we share them with. But remember, just because someone rejects what you offer doesn't automatically mean that it's inferior, useless or of poor value.

They just lack interest. Furthermore, it could mean that you are focusing your energy in the wrong direction. Remember, *be selective*. There's a niche and market for every product offered. There's a person somewhere that's interested in your ideas, beliefs and desires. Your responsibility is to find that person(s).

On the other hand, you *also* have the right to reject that which isn't of interest to you. It's better for you to reject something than to perpetrate a lie. If you're not interested, just be honest. People will appreciate you for your honesty.

2. *Somewhat Important:* There are many circumstances when you may accept something--not because it's the highest priority to you--but because you respect the one who's offering it. For example, a friend may be launching a new makeup line or pursuing a career in photography. You may not be readily interested in what your friend is offering, but because you have mutual respect and endearment for this person, you support their efforts. That's what friends are for, right?

It's easy to support a friend because your friend should be someone that shares the same values as you. If you have been selective in your friendships and relationships, you won't have a conflict when a friend comes to you asking for support. Since you share common values with your friends, it's easy to help them achieve good success as well.

The people in my circle are trustworthy individuals. I don't have to worry about my friends pursuing ventures that will conflict with my good success. Moreover, since I honor and respect them, I too operate from a place of integrity and will never try to engage them in any activity that will hinder good success.

But here's the other side of the coin. When you have a mutual understanding with friends and family, grace plays an important role in the well-being and balancing of these relationships. Friends don't fall out with each other because something isn't prioritized as high on your list as it is theirs. There are times when you won't be able to support them. Maybe what they're asking isn't a high priority for you. Perhaps you have a prior engagement. Perhaps you have higher regard for another relationship. Whatever the reason is, a true friend will give you the grace to say, "No."

3. *Very Important/Emergency:* Some relationships and priorities are preeminent. These relationships include a husband and wife, a parent and child, allegiance to a sibling, and of course, your relationship with God. Some relationships are uncompromising. For example, outside of my relationship with God, the relationship no other between me and my wife is of highest priority. My children are very important, and my ministry assignment is highly regarded as well. But my wife is first. What she requires and needs is of utmost urgency. My allegiance to her is non-negotiable. If my wife needs me, her needs are met first, regardless of what I may have committed myself to prior. There is no prior engagement or commitment that I can have with anyone else that will make me leave my wife in a place of need. She always has an emergency status with me.

Above my relationship with my wife is my relationship with God. But because of my relationship with God, I can honor my wife the way she deserves. Because of my relationship with God, I can be a good parent and friend. My objective is good success; therefore, I strive toward this goal in all areas. We all need a solid relationship with God. As we commit to God, He commits to our good success. As we are devoted to God, He helps us maintain every other important area in our lives. It would be unwise for me to put anyone before God, for He is the one that keeps everything together. Serving as a faithful servant to God should be the most urgent task that we have. Serving God should be a literal emergency for you.

Preacher, author and entrepreneur Mark Moore, Jr. says that we all have what he calls a *master status*. In addition, we have multiple statuses. He talks about how he has a status as a male, a college graduate, a preacher, a son, etc. He concludes, however, that his master status is that of a man of God. Everything in his life is filtered through this status. Because he prides himself on being a man of God, he conducts himself with integrity in business, ministry and relationships. We should approach our lives the same way. Filter your pursuits and relationships through your *master status*.

In this context, our primary goal is good success. Therefore, we must operate with that goal in mind. Only that which is aiding you in accomplishing this goal should be considered urgent. Ask yourself, "Will it help me have good success?" If not, you need to be okay with declining, when necessary.

Do Not Conform

The world defines success one way, and God defines it another. Conventional success is certainly not a bad thing. it's rarely satisfied. The foundation upon which conventional success is sought after is weak. It chases after things, prestige and power. Whereas good success is God-centered and Kingdom-driven. Good success is obtained by those who focus more on giving than receiving.

When a person makes good success their focus, many of the benefits of conventional success will follow—material possessions, prestige and power. It's not that these things are inherently evil. The problem arises when these desires are the principal aim. When you seek after status and wealth first, you almost always end up compromising your moral values and godly principles. Most often, a person conforms to the patterns of society opposed to those outlines by God.

Romans 12:2 (AMP) says, *And do not be conformed to this world [any longer with its superficial values and customs], but be transformed and progressively changed [as you mature spiritually] by the renewing of your mind [focusing on godly values and ethical attitudes], so that you may prove [for yourselves] what the will of God is, that which is good and acceptable and perfect [in His plan and purpose for you].*

This scripture encourages us to avoid the common customs of those that are opposite of the Kingdom of God. Since many of us have been conditioned only by this world, the writer encourages us to renew our minds, causing a transformed life and focus. In having a renewed mind and transformed life, we are able to properly follow God's plan and purpose.

Have Good Expectations

One of the reasons people don't experience godly success is because their expectations are too small. Many people settle for less, and never expect anything more. Perhaps, they accept what they've always been given. They figure that if it has sufficed in the past, it will suffice today. Then, **there are those who settle for less because they don't know that more exists.** We've all have been there before. What we didn't know caused us to miss out on good success.

One of the worst places to be is in the place of regret. Moreover, the saddest commentary is that of those who say, "I wish I knew then what I know now. My life would be so much better right now." However, the one positive thing we can take from this is that now that we know better, it is never too late to do something great. This will begin with expectations, *good expectations*.

When you follow God's blueprint, you are following the blueprint of the master builder. The tallest skyscrapers, the most beautifully constructed monuments, and the most advanced technology can't compare to what God is building with your life. His plan is simply the best. Therefore, in following His design for success, you won't settle for anything less because you know what good success looks like. When I follow God's plan, I expect success. I expect to experience victory. I expect that good things will happen for me. This allows me to build with confidence. It also teaches me how to be selective on a daily basis.

When you have good expectations, you won't follow after anything that impedes your progress. Your expectation of good success will give you the focus to *only* accept opportunities that will assist with that aim. Furthermore, it will teach you how to respond in various situations. This is key because many people lose composure and focus when faced with obstacles. They lose sight of the expectation of success. I believe this is why we're encouraged to walk by faith and not by sight.

Faith keeps you in a place of expectancy. Faith doesn't allow you to entertain anything that doesn't align with your goals. If what I am experiencing isn't what God promised me, then it's only temporary. If God tells you that you are going somewhere, but somehow along the way your vehicle makes a stop, you aren't at your destination yet. Rest assured. Your journey is not over.

...there are those who settle for less because they don't know that more exists.

#GOODSUCCESSBOOK

THE SECOND "S" – SELECTIVE (BE SELECTIVE)

Don't get discouraged where you. Don't get distracted and preoccupied with where you are today. If where you are is not the place God predestined for you, maintain your good expectation, and keep moving forward. You don't have to settle. You don't have to compromise. Stay focused and committed to the plan.

Chapter Eight

THE THIRD "S" – SALVATION

Growing up in church, I sat through many services that consisted of people sharing personal testimonies of what God did for them. We referred to this as "testimony service". Also, during this time, the saints, as we call them, sang a quick song right before they testified. One of my fondest memories is the song that said, "I'm so glad the Lord saved me. If it had not been for Jesus, where would I be? I'm so glad that the Lord saved me." These individuals understood that without God saving them, their lives would be quite different.

No matter what you amass in life, despite your many accomplishments, the greatest success is to know Christ as your Savior. The greatest success comes from being delivered from a life of sin and the effects thereof. Good success is inconceivable without salvation.

Why Salvation?

The call to salvation in this book is deeper than a religious encounter. My aim here is to help you recognize that the greatest love has been made available to you. That love is the love of God.

John 3:16 (ESV) reminds us, *God so loved the world, that He gave His only Son, that whoever believes in Him should not perish but have everlasting life.* Jesus, the Son of God, because of this great love, gave His life so that you and I would have salvation from sin and have eternal life.

I've heard many arguments as it relates to salvation. Many people question why it's even necessary. "Why didn't Got just forgive us?" they ask. The answer is found in the following explanations:

God has given mankind freewill: Books like this wouldn't be necessary if God hadn't given us freewill. If we didn't have freewill, God could simply make us do what He wants. But just because God has given us freewill doesn't mean we are free from the consequences of error. Freewill is simply the

ability to make a choice. Every decision has a consequence, good or bad.

Therefore, after creating the first man and woman, God gave them freedom and dominion. They had the entire world at their feet. They were to rule and preside over this world, and they were meant to prosper and flourish here. In addition to all of the freedom made available to them, they were given guidelines. If they overstepped the guidelines, they suffered negative consequences. They had freewill to choose. This is no different than any other structures set in place today. There are governing rules everywhere. For example, if you receive a driver's license, you have the freedom to drive. However, there are guidelines and rules set in place by the governing authorities to help protect those who will operate vehicles with their newfound freedom. If you cross those boundaries, there will be adverse outcomes.

Adam and Eve, unfortunately, found themselves operating outside of the guidelines of God. As a result, sin and disobedience was introduced into the world. Jesus became a man to satisfy the offense made by Adam and Eve.

His manhood satisfied the earthly debt, while his heavenly DNA allowed His sacrifice to be effective. Man created the offense; therefore, a man was required to satisfy the debt owed. However, only God has the power to forgive sin. So as a man, Jesus was able to be the earthly sacrifice needed to cover sin. As the Son of God, He had the power to forgive and wash sins away.

The entire Bible tells the story of the journey of God's people and how it led us to the eventual death, burial and resurrection of Jesus Christ, the Messiah. The idea of a Messiah is not just a New Testament phenomenon, as some argue. Christ, the Messiah, can be traced through both the Old and New Testament. He was manifested in many situations, and He was there from the foundation of the world.

Because God's love for creation is so strong, He made the way possible for us to return to rightful fellowship with Him. Jesus Christ made the way. In John14:6, Jesus echoes these words, *"I am The Way, The Truth, and The Life. No man comes to the Father but by me."*

...THE GREATEST SUCCESS IS TO KNOW CHRIST AS YOUR SAVIOR.

#GOODSUCCESSBOOK

How Was Good Success Attainable Prior to Salvation?

In the beginning of this book, we confirmed that our individual assignments will vary and it's important to seek God for direction on how to fulfill those assignments. This statement is even relative to how good success was obtained in times past, as well as today. The principle of obedience and honoring God remains; however, some of the actions are different.

Joshua's journey and leadership played a major role in where we as God's people are today. Had it not been for the contributions of people like Moses, Joshua and many other men and women in the Bible, we wouldn't have access to God as we do today. Their actions and obedience to God was counted as good. They achieved good success. Furthermore, their good success set the stage for Christ to do what He came to earth to do--redeem mankind and restore our fellowship with God. Today, we have unfiltered fellowship with God, and this was made possible only through Jesus Christ.

Prior to the life, death and resurrection of Christ, mankind was not able to experience the fullness of God. Thanks to Jesus Christ, good success is much more attainable. In Joshua's day, it was all about observing and keeping the law to please God. By following the laws established by God through Moses, the people of God at that time were able to maintain structures established by God. While many people fell short in this area, those who kept the laws experienced good success. These people had to mind God in all areas of their lives in order to have good success, just as we do. However, when Jesus came along, He became the fulfillment of the law (see Matthew 5:17).

The law, as Paul describes in Galatians, was the *schoolmaster,* our teacher, to lead us to Christ. The law exposed our areas of weakness as it relates to God's standards, helping us to realize that we need divine help to please God. Therefore, through faith in Christ, we gain that missing link to become fully righteous. Now that Christ has died and risen, righteousness can only come through Christ. Through Christ, we now have His Spirit to lead us in the way of truth. We are no longer bound by a long list of laws. God's spirit is our guide, teaching us and reminding us of God's Word, catapulting us to experience good success. As long as we follow the leading of God's Spirit, we will be lead in the way of righteousness.

Good success has always been wrapped up in Jesus Christ. However, it wasn't until His death and resurrection that the gift was unwrapped. In Joshua's day, he obtained good success by pursuing the gift (Christ). In present day, we obtain good success by possessing the gift and appreciating the gift. Our obedience to God is no longer due to the law; it is now due to love. We live for God, not because He requires it, but because we love Him. That's the difference Christ makes.

Benefits of Salvation

Salvation is deliverance. The power of deliverance can be applied to all areas of our lives. One of the great misnomers in our day is that Jesus died for our spiritual man only. While it is true, His primary reason for dying was to make us alive again spiritually. The physical side of our nature benefited, as well. Isaiah 53:5 shows us that not only was Jesus wounded for our transgressions, bruised for our transgressions, and chastised for our peace; with His stripes, we are healed. His stripes not only brought us spiritual healing but also access to physical healing.

The power that was released to the apostles of old by Jesus Christ allowed them to walk in boldness and power, preaching the Word of God and performing miracles of healing and deliverance. It is that same power that is made available for us today to not experience a spiritual awakening, but a physical manifestation of God's power. What God does inwardly is revealed outwardly. Therefore, we have access not only to deliverance spiritually. But we can also believe God for mental deliverance, physical deliverance, financial deliverance and emotional deliverance. We can believe God for deliverance in all areas of our lives. It is God's purpose and will that we who trust Him lack no good thing.

Through salvation, we are made free. We are free to be who God created us to be, and we are free to experience His bountiful pleasures. We are able to have good success because of the power of God made available through Jesus Christ. It's impossible to experience good success if we aren't in right fellowship with God. Salvation brings us from the pit of darkness and brings to the table of light and satisfaction, whereby we are able to enjoy sweet fellowship with the Father.

If you have yet to accept Christ as your Savior, please do so today. Don't do it simply because you desire good success and prosperity in your life. Do it because a relationship with

Jesus Christ is the greatest decision anyone can make. Link up with a strong body of believers that can help you learn and grow. This is called the church, an institution governed by Christ to help us all grow in grace and continue in good success.

In this day, one of the vital conduits to good success that God has provided is the church. The church has been established by God through Jesus Christ, and is necessary for us to be who God has called us to be. In order to understand the importance of the church, it is imperative to define what the church is, why it was established, as well as how it will help us have good success.

The Church

The church can be defined simply as the body of Christ, a group of people who have allegiance to the belief, teachings and leadership of Jesus Christ as the Son of God. The church is comprised of a group of disciples who are committed to the belief that Jesus was born, died and rose again for the salvation of mankind. These disciples go out and share this message with others.

For believers, the church serves as a training ground, helping those who have accepted the faith to maintain their belief in God. Hebrews 10:25 lets us know that we are to strengthen and encourage each other by continued fellowship with each other. The church is to be an example of God's grace and salvation. Moreover, the church is to be a light in a dark and lost world.

Believers find refuge amongst other believers. Furthermore, believers are taught how to be successful in their daily walk with God. The church provides an outlet for believers to learn, grow and have fellowship with like-minded people. With Christ as the head of the church, believers are safe from the attacks of the enemy. We are guaranteed godly success if we remain faithful to God. Jesus said in Matthew 16:18 that He has established the church and the gates of hell will not prevail against it.

The Necessity of the Church

Every week, millions gather to honor and worship God at a place that many refer to as *church*. Church is more than a building; it's who we are as disciples of Christ. The Church is the body of Christ. However, the idea of church as a place helps us see the necessity of *The Church* in a deeper way. Think about what takes place at a church service. There is prayer (unified communication with God). This is a time where we are able to express our sincere sentiments of gratitude and thanksgiving to God through song, praise and worship. Church services almost always include a sermon on a subject that is conducive to godly success.

With everything that takes place each week during church services, many believers couldn't imagine life without church. Many would be lost as it pertains to not only what God requires of us, but also what He has made available to us through Jesus Christ. In essence, it would be impossible to have good success today without the contributions of *The Church*. Because The Church directs us to God, we are able to deeper understand the concept of good success.

Prior to accepting Christ and believing in Him as the Son of the God and the Savior of the world, I was ignorant to the definition of true success. I thought success hinged solely upon my ability to amass money and garner notoriety in my daily pursuits. I thought if I accomplished enough good things, and was connected to the right people, I would be successful. While there is nothing wrong with these things, I left God out of the equation. I pursued riches instead of righteousness. I wanted prestige but I lacked peace. Recognizing who Jesus is, and accepting Him into my life, changed my whole life for the better. Just as the saints would say at my old church while singing in testimony, "If it had not been for Jesus, where would I be?" I wouldn't be where I am today if it had not been for Jesus. Without Christ, we wouldn't be able to experience good success. I'm so glad that the Lord saved me.

Chapter Nine

LIVING THE GOOD SUCCESS LIFE

My desire is for you to be full of God by way of His Word, His love, His peace, His joy and His prosperity. Good success is not just experiencing success at times; it is being *full* of success. Everyone has experienced success at certain points in their lives. But to *be* successful means to live a life of success—*good success*.

By now, you have a good understanding of what good success entails. You are determined to live the good success life. With this newfound determination to honor God with your life, and experience the kind of success that only comes from Him, I want to pose a challenge. This challenge will require you to be intentional and consistent about forthcoming actions. Here's the challenge: Make sure your actions match your desires. It's amazing how many people are satisfied with simply making declarations of what they will become and have. However, good success requires that you live what you say. It's good to "decree and declare," but you must *decide* and *do* if you're going to live the good success life. As the old adage goes, "Practice what you preach."

Don't Just Post It; Live It

Not only should you *practice what you preach*, you must *practice what you post*. In most professions, it is almost necessary to have a strong social media presence. Your presence on social media can really expand your reach. It allows people to engage with you on a different level. However, with the great advantages social media can provide, it's essential that your message lines up with what you're delivering. Many speakers for example, focus on making profound statements and posting inspirational pictures and quotes. Unfortunately, while many of these quotes and statements are posted, everyone posting such content isn't mirroring that in their daily lives. In short, their lives don't match their posts.

This can very well be the case with anyone who has goals, aspirations and dreams. People post things that they themselves simply are not following through on. Again, don't just post it; live it. Don't simply post about wanting a large and lavish home; work to get it. Don't post deep thoughts and quotes about business, relationships and success, but fail to take the necessary steps to flourish in those areas. Make sure your walk matches your posts.

A wise man once told me, "Don't be a public success and a private failure." In other words, don't portray yourself as something that you're not. As Eric Thomas, Ph.D. says, "People will eventually find out that you are not who say you are." Am I suggesting that you post all of your failures and make mention of all your struggles? Absolutely not. However, don't be fake. If you have issues, that's fine. Who doesn't? However, the key is to be authentic. Be yourself.

Be Yourself

One of the biggest challenges humanity faces is not feeling adequate or self-sufficient. Millions of people struggle with negative thoughts and distorted perspectives about themselves. Many question whether they're good enough. Whether it's having a healthy and happy relationship, obtaining that dream job, or having a successful business, people question their adequacy. Most importantly, people question their commitment to God.

As a result of these unfavorable thoughts, many opt to disguise themselves as someone they are not. Moreover, their pursuits and goals aren't fulfilling nor will they help them fulfill their purpose. As a result, they void their good success. When you have conflicting views of yourself, you will settle for a less-than life. In order to avoid this trap, you must believe in yourself. Believe in your gifts. Believe in your purpose.

Self-confidence is the first step to being you. You cannot be successful if you're living someone else's life. No matter how successful a person may be, your success hinges upon your ability to be true to your purpose. You can gain much fame and riches, but if it is at the expense of your purpose, that's not good success. That's not greatness. Good success comes from fulfilling your God-given purpose.

In order to have the God-type of success, you must be yourself and embrace your purpose. In order for you to do either of these, you must embrace God's plan for your life.

Because your purpose and good success are intertwined, it's mandatory to embrace your purpose. To avoid being redundant, we can sum purpose up as: passion mixed with gifts. This mixed with unsolved problems then leads to purpose.

Whether we know it or not, God has given us gifts to fulfill our life's purpose. Our gifts, talents and skills are not just for our benefit, but also for the benefit of others. God has deposited something in you that will be used to make someone else's life better. The final product of good success is making an impact in the world, and our gifts allow this to happen. Our gifts are the proverbial keys that unlock the doors to accomplish our purpose. Furthermore, our gifts help us to not only satisfy our various passions, but they also help us in solving problems in the world.

After Hurricane Katrina, many gifted recording artists banded together and put on a huge concert. The concert featured some of the biggest names in music from various genres. These artists all identified that there was a problem and they were passionate about helping solve that problem. They mixed their passion to help people together with their musical gifts, and solved the problems of many people. The concert raised over 50 million dollars, helping thousands of people. In everything that we do, remember the end goal is to impact lives. Therefore, when pursuing your passions, be certain that lives can be sincerely impacted. There is no good success if other people aren't being impacted by your success.

Love

Love is necessary in order to live the good success life. Love is the glue that binds this whole idea of good success together. We can experience good success because God loves us enough to make it available. Also, because of our love for God, we can experience the many benefits of good success. Without love, none of this would be available. Love is our greatest responsibility and must be embodied by those hoping to achieve and maintain good success.

In Matthew 22, Jesus has a dialogue with a young man who asks Jesus which of the commandments are the greatest. Jesus responds in verses 37 – 40 with these words:

> *"Thou shalt love the Lord thy God with all thy heart, and with all thy soul, and with all thy mind. This is the first and great commandment. And the second is like unto it, Thou*

shalt love thy neighbour as thyself. On these two commandments hang all the law and the prophets."

Love is the greatest commandment. Without love for God, you cannot love each other. Without love for each other, you cannot claim to love God. The two both work hand in hand. The Bible puts it this way in 1 John: *"Beloved, let us love one another, for love is from God, and whoever loves has been born of God and knows God. Anyone who does not love does not know God, because God is love"* (1 John 4:7, 8). The writer goes on to say in the following verses, *"If anyone says, 'I love God,' and hates his brother, he is a liar; for he who does not love his brother whom he has seen cannot love God whom he has not seen. And this commandment we have from him: whoever loves God must also love his brother* (1 John 4:20, 21).

Love God, and love each other. This is the separation between conventional success and good success. Good success causes you to be selfless and concerned about the well-being of someone other than yourself. After experiencing good success yourself, you should desire to share that success with others. Your intention should be to help others experience what you experience.

Choose Good Success

In order to live the good success life, you must choose to do so. Good success requires the conscious, deliberate decision to be successful God's way. Like Joshua said, *"Choose this day who you will serve..."* Joshua echoed these words to the people of God to make a decision to either live for God, or live by the standards of the world. In other words, you have options, but you must choose what you will do. Will you choose to have a mundane, simple success? Or will you choose to experience the thriving, prosperous, godly success. I choose the God kind of success. I'm sure you will do the same.

LOVE IS OUR GREATEST RESPONSIBILITY AND MUST BE EMBODIED BY THOSE HOPING TO ACHIEVE AND MAINTAIN GOOD SUCCESS.

#GOODSUCCESSBOOK

Chapter Ten

SHARE THE WEALTH

Good success is infectious. It's like disease that spreads abroad and grows with each day. Good success is a good disease to have. It causes you to have dis-ease for anyone who has not experienced the joys of this success themselves. After tasting the sweet fruit of good success, you want to share it with others. Like a restaurant that you visit that serves excellent food, you tell everyone about it. You share it with friends. You post reviews about the experience, and you even spread the good news throughout social media. Good success is the same way. Be sure to share the wealth. Don't keep it all for yourself. In fact, the wealthiest person in the world isn't the one who has accumulated the most; it is the one who has shared the most. The more you share, the wealthier you become.

The Responsibility of Good Success

From everyone who has been given much, much will be demanded; and from the one who has been entrusted with much, much more will be asked (Luke 12:48 NIV). Because you have been awarded with such great wealth in good success, you are expected to steward it wisely.

You are required to make an impact with what has been given to you. In addition, God requires that you multiply and increase even that which has been given to you. For Joshua, it was teaching others what he knew. After Jesus came, the disciples were charged to go out and make more disciples. We must view ourselves as disciples of good success. We have a responsibility to spread this knowledge with others.

Consider the parable of the talents. This biblical story is a great representation of responsibility and the importance of stewardship. Found in Matthew 25:14-30, the story exhibits the behavior of the three servants. Each servant was entrusted with the responsibility of stewarding over the talents (money) they received. Although these servants received money, the principles in this parable can be applied to anything good we receive.

Each servant received a different number of talents according to their various abilities. As revealed in the story, they were expected to increase those talents. Two of three servants did as was expected of them. However, one of the servants finished with what he originally received. He wasn't responsible with his talent. As a result, he was unable to enjoy the benefits of good stewardship.

Good success is a gift which we must be good stewards of. If we fail to do this, we risk losing out on the continued benefits of good success. You can't be successful by God's standards without constantly increasing in the gift that He gives you. Mark Moore, Jr. says, "God doesn't just give gifts. He invests them." What God gives you is meant to grow. Be faithful over the gift that God has entrusted to you.

The world is depending on you to do your part, and do it well. Be responsible with your success. Share it with the world so that they too may experience good success.

LIST SOME WAYS YOU WILL SHARE WHAT YOU HAVE LEARNED WITH OTHERS

...THE WEALTHIEST PERSON IN THE WORLD ISN'T THE ONE WHO HAS ACCUMULATED THE MOST; IT IS THE ONE WHO HAS SHARED THE MOST.

#GOODSUCCESSBOOK

About the Author
DeAndre Riley - D.R. Speaks

Everybody has something to say—but not everyone makes an impact with their words. DeAndre Riley, also known as D.R. Speaks, is a multi-faceted force in and out of the four walls of the church. After suffering the loss of both biological parents at a young age, D.R. Speaks made poor decisions that could have destroyed his future. Instead of allowing those things to defeat him, he used them as stepping stones to his unmerited success. As a minister, motivational speaker and author, he seeks to deposit a simple, yet profound principle in the lives of those he may come in contact with: inspire, inform, instruct, and impact.

After his return from college at Michigan State University, D.R. Speaks was immediately thrust into the ministry of his then home church, Bailey Temple Church of God in Christ. Soon after he accepted the call, he was called up and out. While teaching and preaching at various churches throughout the metropolitan Detroit area and surrounding suburbs, he was shaped into a phenomenal orator and servant. It was through his creative ability to dissect the Word of God and teach others how to apply it to everyday life that he discovered his purpose and passion—helping others lead, grow and serve in their God-given purpose.

As the founder of D.R. Speaks Enterprises, he provides motivational speaking and consulting to ministries, organizations, business professionals and corporations. His sole belief that words are the greatest tool given to mankind to aid them in living the life they are destined to live has opened numerous doors of opportunity. In addition, DeAndre is the founder of Man Up Empowerment, Inc. This is a Christian based men's organization focused on empowering and uplifting men to live lives of significance and impact.

He is the founder and pastor of Strive Church in Detroit, MI. This vibrant and relevant ministry is his biggest passion, as he aims to share the love and power of Christ with everyone he comes in contact with. His wisdom, charisma and knowledge speaks for itself—long before he ever speaks a word. D.R. Speaks resides in Michigan. He is married to the love of his life Porsha, and is the father of three wonderful children, DeAndre Jr., Darren Marvin, and Serenity Michelle.

For more information or for booking, please visit www.drspeaks.org

Stay Connected with D.R. Speaks

Social Media
- Facebook.com/DRileySpeaks
- Twitter: @DRileySpeaks
- Instagram: @DRileySpeaks

#DRspeaks #GoodSuccessBook

Website: www.DRspeaks.org

Email: info@drspeaks.org

For information about Strive Church, visit www.StriveChurch.org

www.ingramcontent.com/pod-product-compliance
Lightning Source LLC
Chambersburg PA
CBHW071122090426
42736CB00012B/1984